The Big Flood

Glenreagh 1950

Stories of Heroism and Survival

The Big Flood
Glenreagh 1950

Stories of Heroism and Survival

Compiled by the Local Community in Glenreagh, NSW

Including
Poetry by Charles Dun
Recollections by former residents
Illustrations by Honi Reifler

Edited by Honi Reifler

Nenge Books

The Big Flood Glenreagh 1950 - Stories of Heroism and Survival

Copyright © Glenreagh School of Arts 2023

All rights reserved.

Apart from any use as permitted under the Copyright Act 1968, no part of this book may be reproduced by any process without prior written permission of the copyright holder.

Permission is given for fair copying of selected pages for use by schools or other academic, historic or cultural entities in accordance with copyright rules where an original book has been purchased. The following acknowledgement should be included with the copy: "Excerpt from 'The Big Flood Glenreagh 1950: Stories of Heroism and Survival', ISBN 978-0-6456758-8-7, published by Nenge Books 2023. Copied by permission."

Published by Nenge Books, Australia, May 2023
ABN 26809396184
Email: nengebooks1@gmail.com
Web: www.nengebooks.com

Design and desktop by Nenge Books.
Edited by Honi Reifler.
Illustrations © Honi Reifler 2023.
Jimmy Fisher painting © Lyn Whitmore 1970.
Poem 'Ballad of The Flood' © Charles Dun 2023.
Photographs © Zettie Carten 2023.

This book can be purchased from Glenreagh School of Arts, directly from the publisher at www.nengebooks.com or ordered through booksellers.

Nenge Books publishes quality books using Print-on-Demand (PoD) technology, and ebooks, to assist independent authors publish their work.

ISBN 978-0-6456758-8-7

Dedication

To Zettie.

An integral member of the Glenreagh community who willingly shares her story of the flood to all who ask. Her smiling face lights up in the retelling of this harrowing event.

Contents

Preface	9
Acknowlegements	11
Ballad of The Flood	13
The Rescue of the Darwin Family	26
Memories of Jimmy Fisher	29
Zettie's Postscript	31
Zettie's Name	32
The Chapman Brothers	33
The Elks' Family Experience	34
Alec Pont's Bank	39
Glenreagh Area During The Flood	40

Preface

The Orara River usually flows peacefully through the Orara Valley past Glenreagh in north eastern NSW. But at times it can be a raging torrent. Landowners, especially those with river frontage, respect the river's vagaries. However, no previous experience had prepared the residents for the assault on the night of the 24th June 1950 when the biggest flood in living memory occurred.

Rain had fallen intermittently throughout the month of June, and therefore the valley was very wet. Residents realised when they woke on that Friday morning, with the rain still coming down heavily, that a major flood was a strong possibility. The river was monitored closely all day with people living in the danger areas alerted, animals released from riverside paddocks, and people and precious household items were evacuated to the School of Arts for safety.

Even with this careful preparation, there were many life-threatening situations during that disastrous night. This book is a compilation of some of those stories - the terror, the danger, the response of a small isolated community and the bravery of many - ensuring no human life was lost.

Since that event in 1950, whenever there is any hint of a flood, the old-timers' memories are refreshed and one particular heroic feat is retold to any newcomers who care to listen. Jimmy Fisher's unselfish, brave action is still remembered by many in the Glenreagh community. As memories fade, this book is a record of some of the stories of that pivotal event.

Honi Reifler
Glenreagh
April 2023

Acknowlegements

We gratefully acknowledge Elizabeth Webb's historical work, 'GLENREAGH - A Town of Promise', (1988), as a reference for some of the stories here.

Also, in 1983, Grade 5 and 6 students at Glenreagh Public School interviewed older residents in the community to better understand their history. The project was coordinated by Wilma Towells, who was the teacher. Funded under a Disadvantaged Schools Grants application, the tapes were handed over to the Glenreagh Museum and subsequently transcribed to maintain this oral history as a written record, sections of which have also contributed to the stories in this book.

Other significant contributions to this book are:

"Ballad of The Flood" by Charles Dun;

The painting of Jimmy Fisher by Lyn Whitmore;

Correspondence by Norma Cupitt;

Interviews with Zettie Carten by Honi Reifler;

Photographs by Zettie Carten.

All are used by permission with thanks.

This book has been commissioned by the Glenreagh School of Arts to coincide with the 2023 'Cedar & Steam' annual Glenreagh Art & Photo Exhibition.

Ballad of The Flood

Three days solid rain came down
The Orara River flowed by Glenreagh town.
On June the 29th 1950
a mighty storm hit and the river rose quickly.

Constable Cornford, with two young blokes,
raised the alarm and helped farming folks
moving cattle and stock to ground that was higher.
On people's safety they did enquire.

After helping the Darwin family
they were invited for a cup of tea.
Eight people in all, from young to old,
sat by the lounge room fire to ward off the cold.

Zettie and her mother to the kitchen did go,
when to their horror water did show.
It was coming in through the door
as the river rose and the rain did pour.

The Constable made a hasty decision,
as the river banks burst and the water had risen.
"Open the doors and windows, let the waters through".
Then up to the ceiling went all the crew.

Now, getting all to the ceiling above
took a lot of push and shove.
Two elderly aunts went up too,
as gently as the men could do.

Dresses and petticoats they did wear.
Discretion was needed to lift this old pair.
This sight would make one snicker,
trying to cover petticoat and knicker.

Now, Zettie remembered a birthday cake,
so into the attic for food did take.
Blankets and bedding went up as well.
How long they would be there, no one could tell.

They removed some tin in the early light.
What they saw was a scary sight.
Water everywhere, as far as the eye could see,
swallowing land, house and tree.

They saw a man on the railway track, and made it clear,
"Eight of us are all here".
So, as they waited for help to come,
all ate the cake to the very last crumb.

A rowboat, owned by one Ned Chapman,
was taken through the pouring rain.
To the river's edge they heaved and lifted,
as the flood waters swirled and shifted.

To save these souls, who would row
through the raging torrent's twist and flow?
The only one to raise his hand
was Jimmy Fisher, an Aboriginal man.

As Jimmy pushed out from the shore,
with all his strength, he manoeuvred each oar.
He arrived at 10am at the Darwin's, and called in a tone,
knocking the roof and called, "Is there anyone home?"

When they saw his face, hope was detected.
From death to life, like Christ resurrected.
Jimmy had some rum for all to share,
he was there to save and there to care.

When Constable Crawford showed his face,
the rum was hidden at a very quick pace,
as Aboriginals were not allowed to drink,
and this could land Jimmy in the clink.

The older women were first to board.
For Jimmy, their safety was assured.
He rowed them all to the waiting crowd,
but Jimmy was spent and his head was bowed.

Exhausted from this mammoth task,
to have a rest was all that he asked.
He was given the rum to drink, and keep,
and recovered after a good long sleep.

Jimmy became a favourite son.
In Glenreagh, he was now a number one.
To go to the pub, permission was given.
A just reward, now his life was worth liven'.

So that is the story of a man that was black,
saving eight people from flood to track.
An Aboriginal, indigenous to this great land,
Jimmy Fisher, a much respected Glenreagh man.

By Charles Dun

The Rescue of the Darwin Family

*H*ere is a fuller description of the rescue of the Darwin family and three men, as researched and recorded by Glenreagh's historian, Elizabeth Webb.

Jimmy Fisher's name was revered in the community of Glenreagh after the big flood of 1950, the biggest flood ever recorded for our lovely Orara River. Jimmy, of indigenous descent, lived near the railway station in a hut owned by the railways, as he worked on the railway line.

Jimmy and other railway workers were standing around near their huts when they heard the news over the radio that the Darwin family were stranded on their roof and were waiting to be rescued. All that could be seen of the house was the roof above the flood waters.

The day before, Constable Cornford, with Max Loy and Allan Green, had gone around the district alerting folk to the danger of rising flood waters. At this stage the traffic bridge across the Orara River was still traffic-able.

It was late in the evening when they called on the Darwin family, using torches to get the cattle to the safety of higher ground. With this accomplished, they were all soon seated around a big open fire in the lounge room talking to the family - Mr and Mrs Darwin, their twenty year old daughter, Zettie[1], as well as Mrs Darwin's two elderly sisters.

Zettie remembers that all was well until she and her mother went into the kitchen to get refreshments and noticed that floodwater was already creeping across the floor.

They immediately started lifting things onto cupboards and wardrobes. Bedding was placed in the ceiling through the manhole. Constable Cornford opened all the windows and doors so that the water could flow through, rather than running the risk of having the home swept off its blocks. The water rose so quickly that they had to stand on the kitchen table to reach the manhole. It was an effort to get the two aunts up into the ceiling. The final item to be rescued from the flooding house was a birthday cake on the top of the fridge. Mrs Darwin had made the cake to send to her daughter, Lola, at Dorrigo by train the next day.

It must have been a terrifying night for the eight people jammed in the dark ceiling as the flood waters pounded against the house. The fast flowing current, carrying massive amounts of debris and dying animals, crashed against their place of fragile refuge. The plum trees, on the southern side of the house, helped deflect some of the impact of the water as the group waited for daylight.

When they looked out where a sheet of roofing iron had been removed, they were shocked to see water everywhere. A man, walking along the railway line, was hailed and advised that, "All are here!" As they waited for help to arrive, Zettie recalled how hungry they were and she remembered Lola's birthday cake that they had rescued. They appeased their hunger with the cake cut in pieces with the lid of the cake tin.

Jimmy sprang into action when he heard the news that they were waiting to be rescued. He knew that the local publican, Frank Feighen, owned a boat so he set off walking along the railway line, only to find that it was being used to rescue the Elks family further south.

Ned Chapman's boat was available and several townsfolk helped Jimmy carry it across the railway bridge. At this time the water was lapping the sleepers under the bridge and the river was roaring. They lowered the boat into a spot with slightly less turbulent waters, near the savage main current which was thrashing the treetops wildly and filled with fast traveling debris. Tom Chapman remembers that it was Jimmy who stepped forward and took the oars. "A very brave thing to do," were Tom's words.

About 10am those stranded in the flooded house heard a voice calling, "Anyone home?" They were astounded because they were surrounded by flood waters. On looking out from the hole in the roof they became aware of a man in a boat nearby. He brought the boat closer to the house and reached out with a bottle of rum. But, on sighting Constable Cornford, he hurriedly hid the bottle in the boat. (The Laws at that time didn't allow indigenous people to be served drinks in the hotel and Constable Cornford had previously given Jimmy advice about his drinking).

Jimmy asked how many were in the ceiling and when told eight he replied, "I'll take the women first," and proceeded, with help, to steady the boat for loading. It was a nervous effort to get them in the boat but he bravely rowed through the unrelenting flood waters to the safety of the railway line. Many willing hands had gathered to help the ladies out of the rocking vessel. Jimmy collapsed on the bank from sheer exhaustion and was given a drink of rum, with the Constable's blessing.

After Jimmy recovered with sleep, the Constable gave him permission to drink at the hotel anytime he wished, providing someone saw him across the bridge and safely home. Jimmy became one of Glenreagh's favourite people and the Darwin family never forgot Jimmy's efforts in their rescue.

The Darwin family sustained heavy losses in the flood. Only 14 head of cattle had survived but their two horses, pigs and poultry had drowned. They only had the clothes that they were wearing and moved into an aunty's home in the main street. Zettie remembers that, for a long time after the flood, passers-by would often sing the words of a popular song:

> 'When you are up to your neck in hot water,
> Be like the kettle and sing.'

Zettie married Murray Carten in 1965 and they have two children, Garry and Cheryl. She still lives in Glenreagh today and has made a lasting impact in this small community.

Memories of Jimmy Fisher

It has been impossible to track down details of Jimmy Fisher's early life. He was certainly in Glenreagh in 1950, at the time of the big flood, and was working on the railways as a ganger.

A letter from Norma Cupitt (nee Hambly) who grew up in Rappville and then came to Glenreagh as a teacher, gives some details of Jim.

Rappville was a village between Grafton and Glenreagh. It had a hotel, cafe, newsagent, butcher, baker, general store and two churches - Roman Catholic and Anglican. Across the railway line was a hall and the Rappville Public School.

The railway line cut the village in half. There was a well kept Railway Station, with a Station Master and an Assistant Station Master. There was a large paddock next to the Station which was called the Sleeper Paddock where sleepers (timber used in the railway line) were stored. A lot of maintenance of the line was carried out and they brought in what they called an 'Extra Gang'. They were camped in the sleeper yard and used to come across to the shop for their supper.

The Assistant Station Master was a Mr Ferguson and his daughter, Myfanwy, was one of my best friends. Her younger brother, John ('Chika') Ferguson played Rugby League for Canberra. The Ferguson Family were Aboriginal.

Jimmy was on the 'Extra Gang' and he would come to the butcher's shop for his supplies. My father, Clive Hambly, ran the Butcher Shop. Dad spent a lot of time talking to Jimmy, he was very fond of him. They loved yarning. I wish Dad was still around as he knew so much about Jimmy. Jimmy used to tell him about his early years. I don't know where he was born but I suspect it was in the Northern Rivers area. It may have been Tabulum on the Clarence. He would have belonged, I think, to a tribe in that area - possibly YUGUMBAL from the upper reaches of the Clarence or BANDJALONG, between Grafton and Ballina.

Jimmy was a full-blood Aboriginal, a gorgeous man whom we all respected. I would have been 10 or 11 when he was in Rappville working on the Railway…1950-51, around that time.

One conversation Dad was having with him I remember quite well. Dad said to Jimmy, "You are lucky, Jim, you wouldn't get sunburned like we white people. It would be good to have dark skin like you. Sunburn can be so painful."

Jimmy replied, "Don't worry boss, we get sunburned too and it can be really painful."

Rappville was a community where everyone was accepted, we were all treated well no matter what colour our skin was. People had a respect for one another and Jimmy was just one of us.

I don't know where he moved to from Rappville, possibly south on the railway. Workers moved on when their work was completed. I can remember seeing Jimmy at Glenreagh. I went there in 1961 as a teacher (straight out of College).

Zettie's Postscript

Jimmy stayed on in Glenreagh and worked for the railways. Out of thankfulness for Jimmy's heroic action, Claude Darwin invited him to dinner every Wednesday night. At Christmas the family gave him a new shirt, a pair of trousers, shoes and socks. His reply was always, "You shouldn't buy these for me 'cause I don't go anywhere."

He was also given a photo of Zettie in her debut dress, which he treasured.

"I don't know why you're not married!" Jimmy would often say, "I would hang my hat on every post for you".

Sadly, Jimmy passed away in tragic circumstances. He had been living in a small railway house near the line with an open fireplace. When it was noticed that he hadn't been seen for a few days the policeman went to investigate. Jimmy had rolled into the fire and lay there unconscious. He was transported to hospital but died without anyone in Glenreagh being notified. The town couldn't attend his funeral but mourned the loss of a kind, heroic man.

Zettie's Name

Claude Darwin was the first in Glenreagh to enlist for World War I. He was awarded a Distinguished Service Medal for Bravery from the Queen and signed by Winston Churchill for rescuing one of his mates under gunfire. Claude was shot in the neck during this incident and was transported back to Egypt for medical care. He had to sit in a deck chair with his head braced between two bricks for six weeks with a silver ferrule in his neck. He credited his survival to a caring Egyptian nurse, Zettie, and declared that if he ever had a daughter he would call her Zettie.

The Chapman Brothers

This story is composed from conversations that Tom Chapman had with our local historian, Elizabeth (Bessie) Webb.

The rain was heavy and consistent for a few days and on Friday morning, the 24th June 1950, the whole district experienced a really fierce storm. On the Saturday morning Tom decided to walk south of the village to check on his two brothers, Joe and Ned. The local baker walked with him, as did several other folk.

The two brothers lived in wooden homes quite close to the Orara River and bounded by the Glenreagh to Dorrigo railway line. Joe's home had been the administrative office of the railway and was built from a light pine. Ned lived in the bigger home on the property.

Tom arrived in time to see his brother Ned bringing Joe and his wife out of their home. The very bedraggled family arrived to the safety of the higher railway line after swimming and rowing desperately. Just as they set their feet safely on higher ground, they saw Joe's home being swept off its blocks by the raging flood waters. It smashed into the stanchions of the railway bridge, with timber going everywhere. Tom recalled that they were able to rescue the bath, the stove and some timber pieces later on.

Jimmy Fisher knew that the publican owned a boat, but what he didn't know at that time was that it was being used to rescue the Elks family. In his search for the boat he crossed the railway bridge and encountered the people who had just witnessed the Chapman house afloat. Ned Chapman's boat, which he had just used to save some of his family, was there. So Tom and Ned and several other local men assisted Jimmy to carry the boat across the railway bridge, with the water lapping the sleepers under the tracks. The boat was placed in the swollen river at the eastern end of the railway bridge and Jim stepped forward and took the oars…

The Elks' Family Experience

Dorothy Elks was interviewed by the Glenreagh Primary School students in 1983, with her harrowing tale of that fateful night in 1950. Here are some excerpts from her accounts:

Our house was on the banks of the Orara River, just a mile south of Glenreagh. It was on a very high bank… around about 37-40 feet high. My grandfather built the house in 1907. It was a very solid house built from iron and timber. My grandparents came here in 1906 and there hadn't been a flood across that part of the farm before. That area had always been out of the water in all the big floods that had been experienced in the past.

All June 1950 it rained on-and-off and we'd had quite enough when it started to pour again on the 24th. We could see that we were going to have a big flood, so we put all the cattle and horses around the house and we went back to bed.

At around midnight, my husband got up to check the water because it had been raining so heavy. The water was still quite a way from the house, so we went back to bed. But it poured very heavily again and I woke up to the sound of dripping water. It seemed so close, so I got up and the water was nearly up to my knees in the house. My first thought was for the two children in the next room. I ran in and they hadn't woken, thank goodness. The bottoms of their beds were jumping up and down with the wash of the water in the room.

We found a candle and went to the room where the manhole was. My husband pushed a table under the manhole, put a chair on the table and pushed the children up through the manhole. The water came up so quickly that it was around his waist by the time he made it up inside.

We stayed up inside the roof all night. In that time we heard a cow come into the house but it couldn't get out. We could hear her mooing. Later we discovered that she had drowned in the bathroom. When it became daylight my husband found a loose piece of timber that had been left up there and he belted a sheet of tin (roofing iron) off. He called to my parents who

Joan Schulz (nee Ellem) sitting on the traffic bridge over the Orara River at Glenreagh. During the flood the approaches had been washed away and a ladder had to be used to get onto the bridge. This photo would have been taken by her sister Faye Gam (nee Ellem) with her trusty Box Brownie camera.

were in their house on the opposite side of the road at the time. They could hear us calling and as soon as it was daylight, they could see what was happening. Only the roof of our house was sticking out of the water.

My brother, Sam, walked right up the back of the Dorrigo Line and down to Glenreagh so that he could get across the creek. He swam with his hat on his head, because it was raining, he said! He didn't want to take it off and he got into Glenreagh to get help for us. Mr. Feighan (the publican) and his son, Bob, came across in a boat to get us. It was very frightening coming over in that boat with all the water rushing about. The boat turned around a few times and we got caught on a fence post at one stage, but Mr Feighan was so calm. It was so good to see my mum. She was waist deep in water waiting for us to get out of the boat.

We couldn't get back to our house until after lunch on the day of the 26th June. Everything had been washed away - cattle, horses and everything. Over 100 chooks and some dogs had drowned. I had a pet dog that had had a broken leg, which we had splinted. He too was washed away and we never found any sign of him.

The water had come seven foot two inches in the house. Everything was a colossal mess and washed all around, all over the place. It was very heartbreaking to go back and see. We stayed with my parents, in the house opposite, until we got cleaned up. It took a long time to dry the house out. It was very buckled and we had to leave everything open to dry out.

Between then and the 1954 flood, we shifted things out of the house three times thinking it was going to do the same thing again. When the '54 flood came, we left the house before the water went in.

The residents, and everyone around here, said that a flood like the 1950 one hadn't happened in this century, so it wouldn't happen again! But in 1954 it was three feet nine inches in the house. So we decided that we would have the house moved up onto a part of the farm where there would be no flood.

The house from which the Darwin family was rescued was later moved to the eastern side of the railway line. Only the plum trees and a date palm indicate where it once stood. Dorothy Elks recalled moving their home:

After the flood in 1954, they had said that the water wouldn't go over there again. But I couldn't stand the strain. It would get on my nerves every time it rained. So we decided we would have the house moved up onto a part of the farm where there would be no flood.

We got the house put on 'runners' they were called. They were like big poles and Mr Russ senior pulled it with his Alice Chalmers tractor. When they got to the creek it dug in and the tractor got bogged. They then went into Glenreagh and got Mr Howard Wright - he had a big truck at the time - and so, between the timber truck and the tractor, they got the house to where it is now. A local builder, Mr Reid, put the brick blocks under it and Clarrie helped. They jacked it up and they would jack about three inches at a time and put a block under it and start off with the bigger ones and then put a smaller one. I used to crawl underneath the house with buckets of mortar to put between the blocks. We were just so pleased to get the house out of the flood and to feel safe.

Although the Elks family survived the ordeal, most of their animals did not. Only three cows survived out of a herd of twenty four. Because it was winter time, the cows were all rugged against the cold, and the heavy wet rugs meant that they would have had difficulty swimming to safety.

Howard's Ingenuity

After the flood waters receded, the damage to the traffic bridge was revealed. The approaches to both ends of the bridge were washed away and it was impossible to get stones into town to repair the damage.

This was an anxious time for the residents on the eastern side as they couldn't get into the village. It was also troubling for those in the village on the western side as they couldn't get to the railway station. Authorities soon had ladders placed at the ends of the bridge where the approaches had been washed away. The townsfolk climbed the ladders and carried on with life as things struggled to get back to some kind of normality.

But, there was a problem that no ladder could solve for one determined Glenreagh resident. Howard Wright's 1935 Chevrolet car was locked in a shed near the railway line and he decided that he couldn't wait the three months to get the traffic bridge's approaches repaired. He clambered over the make-shift ladders on the traffic bridge and walked to the shed housing his precious car.

Howard let the air out of the tyres, and with a steady hand on the wheel, drove his car onto the railway line. With two men walking in front of him, guiding any wheel movement that might take the car off the line, he drove very slowly across the still flooded Orara River and over the railway bridge to the village side. The railway bridge was two and a half metres higher than the traffic bridge.

Howard was later told that driving a car across the railway bridge, while the river was flooded, couldn't be done. He replied, "I've already done it!" In telling the story in 1987, Howard did recall that it was 'hair raising', but worth doing in order to get the car over. A local resident, Tom Chapman, commented that it was because of Howard's driving ability, and having the nerve to even attempt it in the first place, that he succeeded in accomplishing this amazing rescue.

Alec Pont's Bank

Alec and Dulcie Pont, with their three children, were living on the eastern side of the river in 1950, near the sawmill. They managed to escape from the rising water, but in the morning light they discovered that their house had been lifted from its blocks, twisted around by the force of the water and deposited near the road. Their refrigerator was later found in a tree near the pumping station. Alec, who the family said 'didn't trust the banks', returned to his house site as soon as the water receded. He had always saved any spare money in a golden syrup tin which he hid under the back step. This step was a solid piece of log with a flattened top and was the only thing that remained of the house in that spot. The tin was still there and the money was intact.

Glenreagh Area During The Flood

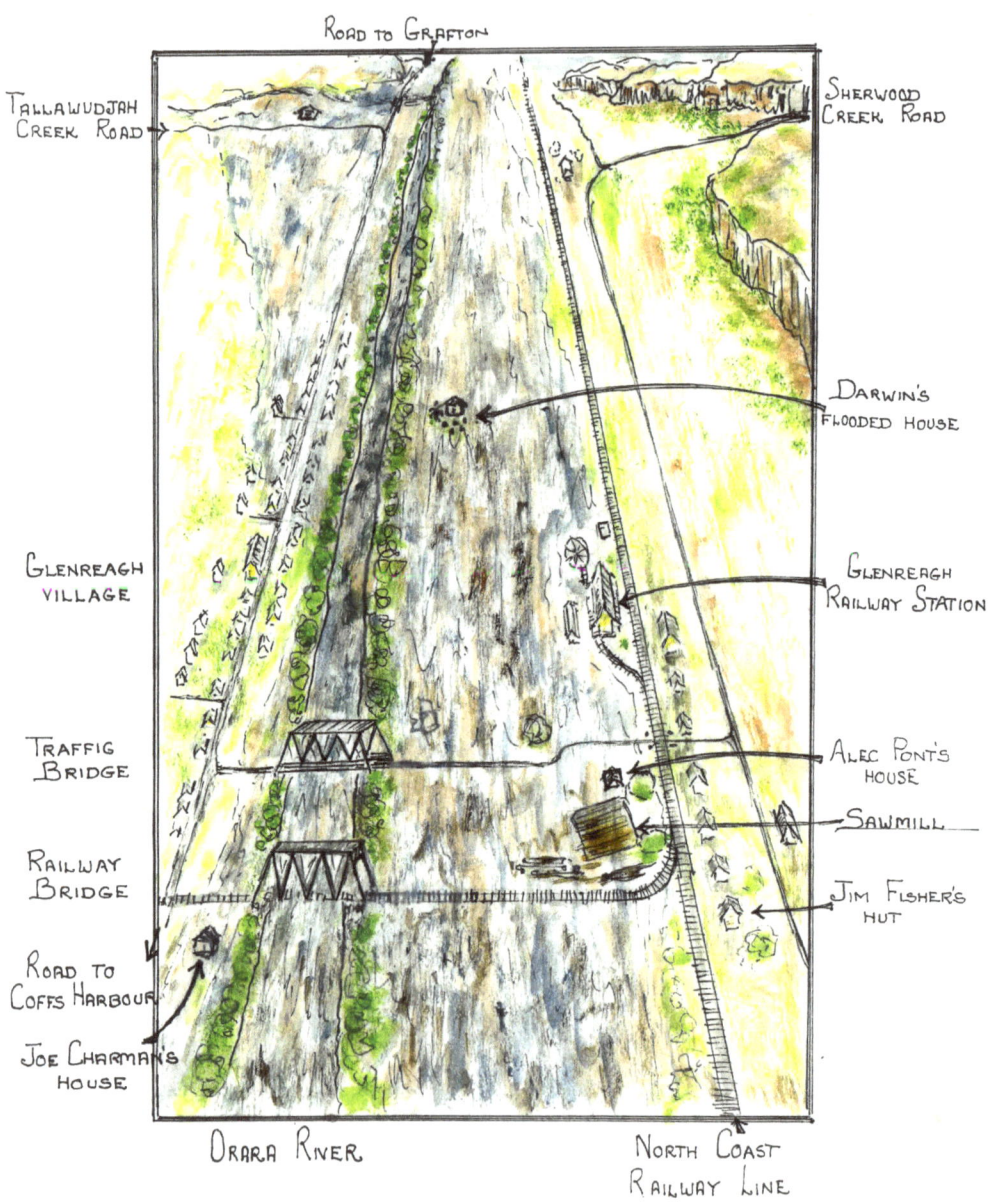

www.ingramcontent.com/pod-product-compliance
Lightning Source LLC
Chambersburg PA
CBHW041431010526
44107CB00046B/1573